especially for

....

from

....

date

....

Praise for *When God Says "Wait"*

"In *When God Says 'Wait'*, Elizabeth captures readers through previously unexplored anecdotes of familiar Bible stories and then connects you with these ancient icons, venturing deeper into their narratives. This book is the culmination of years of grappling with questions and faith-testing waiting with practical insights of the way God works in these times."

–Pauli and Chip Wade, Lead Creative at Wade Works, Star of HGTV's *Elbow Room* and *Curb Appeal*

"*When God Says 'Wait'* is a must-read. Elizabeth gives us confidence and courage in times of waiting, ensuring that we will be 'better because of the wait.' Whether you're a mom, student, business owner, or wife, this book is for you!"

–Lara Casey Isaacson, author of *Make It Happen*

"Elizabeth Thompson is a kindred spirit. I love her writing style, heart, and quirky humor. She writes with authenticity and wisdom. It's a must-read for anyone struggling with God's timetable."

–Andy Lee, author of *A Mary Like Me: Flawed Yet Called*

"It's hard to be the example, but someone's gotta do it! Thank goodness it is Elizabeth—her journey through waiting, wit in expressing it, and wisdom to learn from it. This book is not only a beautiful testament of one woman's faith, but a reminder of the many Bible heroes who God told to wait."

–Laura Whitaker, Executive Director, Extra Special People, Inc.

"As Elizabeth writes, when speed is our cultural priority, 'wait' feels like a bad word. While most authors dealing with such tender topics may shy away from hard-to-swallow truths, Elizabeth guides, challenges, and encourages just like a best friend—with vulnerability and humor—so that your heart can fall deeper in love with a God who sees, hears, and cares."

–Marilisa Schachinger, Founder and Event Planner, Martel Events

When God Says

wait

A Journal

Elizabeth Laing Thompson

When God Says *wait*

A Journal

SHILOH RUN PRESS
An Imprint of Barbour Publishing, Inc.

Member of the
Evangelical Christian
Publishers Association

We're All *waiting* for Something

A job, a true love, a baby, a cure. . . We're all waiting on something from God. And the place between His answers can feel like a wasteland where dreams—and faith—go to die. When we're waiting, we torture ourselves with questions no one can answer: *Why? Why me? How long?*

Waiting is unfamiliar terrain for many of us. New territory. We have forgotten how to navigate it—or maybe we never learned to begin with.

Waiting seasons come in different forms: Some are roller-coaster rides, hurtling us up, down, and all around—*We're getting what we want—just kidding, not getting what we want*; *The Thing is finally happening—nope, not happening at all*; *God is saying yes—just kidding, He's saying no—or maybe He's saying wait—uh, we have no idea what God is saying*. . . The temptation is to suffer through the ride, eyes shut, teeth clenched, fists white-knuckled, whisper-begging, "Tell me when it's over." And then you have the other kind of wait: the quiet kind. Monotonous, stagnant, boring. We're stuck in life's waiting room, where nothing ever happens and nothing ever changes. Life feels useless, meaningless, a song stuck on repeat. Every day the same: same old classes, same old job, same old apartment. How we wish things would change, how we long for the next thing—The Thing we are convinced we cannot be happy without—but change won't come.

Whatever kind of wait you are enduring right now, I pray you find hope and strength in these pages. I have found journaling and meditation to be powerful tools during my waiting seasons. They have helped me to slow the chaos of my thoughts, concentrate on God's Word rather than my own fears or discouragement, and find peace—even joy—in the in-between.

Waiting time need not be wasted life. We can redeem waiting times by giving them to God, so that when our name is finally called and our time in the waiting room is over (*hallelujah*), we can dance out of the waiting room feeling good about how we spent our time there. We might even high-five a few new friends on the way out.

I pray journaling helps you ride out the wait with courage, hope, and a sense of humor. I pray you open your eyes and find joy in the twists and turns, exhilaration in the unknown. No, it won't be fun the whole time. It won't always be peaceful or happy. You'll have moments when you'll wish God had buckled you into a different ride. But if you'll learn to embrace the experience, waiting can be an adventure. A story—*your life story*. A life you do not waste. A life you live in present tense, every day—not just in hindsight, when you know how it all turned out. A life you live to the full, without fear, even now: eyes open, heart unguarded, hands raised to heaven.

When God says, *"Wait,"* He doesn't tell us for how long.

When God says, *"Wait,"* we face one of life's greatest tests.

When God says, *"Wait,"* we have decisions to make.

When God says, *"Wait,"* we can control only two things: how we wait, and who we become along the way.

In this thought journal, I invite you to dive more deeply into your wait. To embrace the questions. Lean into the lessons. Find hope in the heartache. Draw near to the Father who loves you even as He says, *"Wait."*

So. . .what are we waiting for? Let's get started.

~Elizabeth

Trust in the Lord and do good; dwell in the land and enjoy safe pasture. Take delight in the Lord, and he will give you the desires of your heart. . . . Be still before the Lord and wait patiently for him.
Psalm 37:3–4, 7

···

···

···

···

···

···

*F*or many of us, waiting seasons are the first time our faith has been truly tested. They present risk and opportunity in equal measure, making us ask the hard faith questions, making us fight to find—and accept—the answers.

What are you waiting for right now? Are you happy with how you are handling this season of waiting so far? Why or why not?

....

....

....

....

....

....

....

....

....

....

....

....

....

....

....

....

....

....

....

....

All my longings lie open before you, Lord; my sighing is not hidden from you. My heart pounds, my strength fails me; even the light has gone from my eyes. . . . LORD, I wait for you; you will answer, Lord my God.
PSALM 38:9–10, 15

....

....

....

....

....

....

....

....

....

....

....

....

....

....

....

....

....

*N*o matter what kind of wait you are enduring today, be it the soul-killing kind of wait or the daily-joy-stealing kind of wait, hear this, know this: your pain, your doubt, your struggles, your feelings are real. Valid. You have a wound that needs tending.

What's the hardest part about waiting? What questions about faith, God, or God's promises do you need to resolve?

*For this very reason, make every effort to add to your faith goodness;
and to goodness, knowledge; and to knowledge, self-control;
and to self-control, perseverance; and to perseverance, godliness;
and to godliness, mutual affection; and to mutual affection, love.
For if you possess these qualities in increasing measure, they
will keep you from being ineffective and unproductive
in your knowledge of our Lord Jesus Christ.*
2 PETER 1:5–8

....

....

....

....

....

....

....

....

....

....

....

....

....

....

....

*W*hen I'm waiting, I want more than just a *yes* or *no* from God. It's not enough to know *if*; I want to know *when*. I want a timeline. But life doesn't work that way; God doesn't work that way. It is in the *not knowing* that God can work on our heart, our faith, our character.

How is God working on your character through the not knowing?

....

....

....

....

....

....

....

....

....

....

....

....

....

....

....

....

....

....

....

....

Consider it pure joy, my brothers and sisters, whenever you face trials of many kinds, because you know that the testing of your faith produces perseverance. Let perseverance finish its work so that you may be mature and complete, not lacking anything.

JAMES 1:2–4

....

....

....

....

....

....

....

....

....

....

....

....

....

....

....

....

*D*id you catch that nuance in James 1:4—"*Let* perseverance finish its work"—as in it's up to us to allow that work to happen so we can grow? As in trials produce perseverance, and perseverance can lead to spiritual maturity, but we have to *let it happen*, not fight the process? (I know, probably not what you wanted to hear—me neither.) *If we let Him*, God can use our waiting journeys to shape us, to make us into the people He created us to be.

Character is built slowly: step by step, choice by choice, even mistake by mistake, one strength building on another over time. Smack in the middle of this character-building process we find the trait we desperately need when we are waiting: perseverance.

What one character trait would you most like to grow in during your waiting season? What scriptures can help you in developing that trait?

....

....

....

....

....

....

....

....

....

....

....

....

....

For everything that was written in the past was written to teach us, so that through the endurance taught in the Scriptures and the encouragement they provide we might have hope.

ROMANS 15:4

....

....

....

....

....

....

....

....

....

....

....

....

....

....

....

....

....

....

....

*K*nowing our weakness, knowing our need, God offers us many stories of godly people who have wrestled with waiting with varying success.

What Bible character do you most relate to in your wait?
What strengths do you want to imitate in them,
and what can you learn from their mistakes?

....
....
....
....
....
....
....
....
....
....
....
....
....
....
....
....
....
....
....
....

*Therefore the L*ORD *waits to be gracious to you, and therefore*
*he exalts himself to show mercy to you. For the L*ORD *is a God*
of justice; blessed are all those who wait for him.
ISAIAH 30:18 ESV

....

....

....

....

....

....

....

....

....

....

....

....

....

....

....

....

....

....

*T*hrough our waiting seasons, perseverance can gradually "finish" its never-ending work in us. As waiting does its thing, and God does His, we get the chance to become our best selves, the people God designed us to be.

When you look back on this season, how do you want to describe yourself? If you could change one thing about how you're handling this waiting season, what would it be?

....

....

....

....

....

....

....

....

....

....

....

....

....

....

....

....

....

....

....

Finally, be strong in the Lord and in his mighty power. Put on the full armor of God, so that you can take your stand against the devil's schemes. For our struggle is not against flesh and blood, but against the rulers, against the authorities, against the powers of this dark world and against the spiritual forces of evil in the heavenly realms. Therefore put on the full armor of God, so that when the day of evil comes, you may be able to stand your ground, and after you have done everything, to stand.
EPHESIANS 6:10–13

*W*hen we go into spiritual battle, we will need to know where we require special protection—which parts of our spiritual armor have vulnerabilities, or even gaping holes. Satan loves to take advantage of our weaknesses, but God can turn even weakness into strength (see Hebrews 11:34).

Take some time to identify which specific pitfalls are most threatening to you. What scriptures can help you battle those temptations? Here are a few to get you started—bitterness: James 5:7–11; doubt: Psalm 37:25–26, James 5:16–18; manipulation: Psalm 33:11–22, 2 Peter 3:13–15; cynicism: Psalm 40:1–3 (I love The Message *version of this one!); envy: Psalm 73, James 3:13–18.*

....

....

....

....

....

....

....

....

....

....

....

....

....

....

I remain confident of this: I will see the goodness of the Lᴏʀᴅ in the land of the living. Wait for the Lᴏʀᴅ; be strong and take heart and wait for the Lᴏʀᴅ.

Psᴀʟᴍ 27:13–14

....

....

....

....

....

....

....

....

....

....

....

....

....

....

....

....

....

....

I don't know how your waiting story ends—how long you will wait, and will God say yes?—but this I know: you may be sad and struggling now, but God can restore laughter in the end.

He can bring back joy after months, years, even decades of waiting.

He can bring back joy after you have doubted and questioned.

He can bring back joy after you have made mistakes—yes, even the kind with lasting consequences.

He can use your wait to shape you, make you stronger and more Christlike.

Think about a time when you have seen God bring joy and redemption out of heartache. Describe what God did and how you felt.

....
....
....
....
....
....
....
....
....
....
....
....
....
....
....
....

*"Go in peace, and may the God of Israel grant
you what you have asked of him."*

1 SAMUEL 1:17

....

....

....

....

....

....

....

....

....

....

....

....

....

....

....

....

....

....

....

....

If you have already given in to some of waiting's pitfalls, if you are struggling even now as you read, hear this, know this: Your story isn't over. You can stumble and fall, you can question and doubt—and God can help you set it right. You can get the last laugh. Best of all, you can laugh *with God*.

Have you ever laughed with God over a surprising "plot twist"
in your life? Describe what God did and how you felt.

....

....

....

....

....

....

....

....

....

....

....

....

....

....

....

....

....

....

*I wait for the L*ORD*, my soul waits, and in his word I hope; my soul waits for the Lord more than watchmen for the morning, more than watchmen for the morning.*
PSALM 130:5-6 ESV

....

....

....

....

....

....

....

....

....

....

....

....

....

....

....

....

....

....

When you have been waiting forever, you will be tempted to stop praying.

Pray anyway.

You might think, *I've already asked God for this five gazillion times. He must be sick of hearing from me.*

Pray anyway.

You might think, *I have nothing new to say.*

Pray anyway.

Write a prayer in the space below and share what's on your heart with your heavenly Father.

....

....

....

....

....

....

....

....

....

....

....

....

....

....

But as for me, I will look to the Lᴏʀᴅ; I will wait for the God of my salvation; my God will hear me.

Mɪᴄᴀʜ 7:7 ᴇsᴠ

*W*hen you are waiting, you will have despairing days. Days when you want to hole up in your room and huddle in the dark with sad thoughts. Worshipping God, especially in a congregational setting, will feel like the worst idea in the world. How can joyful songs come from a heart riddled with loss?

Don't give in.

Worship will minister to you in ways you don't even know you need. It will fill holes in your soul you don't realize you have, gaps you can't fill yourself.

In what ways has worship been difficult for you during your wait?
In what ways has it ministered to you?

....
....
....
....
....
....
....
....
....
....
....
....
....
....

Look on me and answer, LORD my God.
Give light to my eyes, or I will sleep in death. . . .
But I trust in your unfailing love;
my heart rejoices in your salvation.
I will sing the LORD's praise,
for he has been good to me.
PSALM 13:3, 5–6

....

....

....

....

....

....

....

....

....

....

....

....

....

....

....

....

*W*orship gives us perspective, reminding us that as big as our problems feel, as much as we hurt, there's a whole world out there in need of God. In need of *our faith* to make a difference.

Worship reminds us of the power of God—the power He can exercise on our behalf.

Worship reminds us that God is God and we are not.

Worship helps us understand and accept God's love.

Worship helps us appeal to God even when we don't know how to pray.

Worship helps us heal.

Worship helps us wait.

What do you gain from worship that you can't attain any other way?
List the worship songs that most speak to your heart as you
wait. Make a playlist and listen to those songs often.

....

....

....

....

....

....

....

....

....

....

....

....

....

....

"Come to Me, all you who labor and are heavy laden, and I will give you rest. Take My yoke upon you and learn from Me, for I am gentle and lowly in heart, and you will find rest for your souls. For My yoke is easy and My burden is light."

MATTHEW 11:28–30 NKJV

....

....

....

....

....

....

....

....

....

....

....

....

....

....

....

....

....

....

Waiting can bleed us dry—drain our hope, our happiness, our heart. But God's Word can fill us back up again. If waiting is a desert, then God's Word is the oasis where we pause to refresh our water supply.

What doubts or questions have you struggled with during your wait? What scriptures, godly counsel, and spiritual books can help you work through those questions?

....

....

....

....

....

....

....

....

....

....

....

....

....

....

....

....

....

Because of the Lᴏʀᴅ's great love we are not consumed, for his compassions never fail. They are new every morning; great is your faithfulness. I say to myself, "The Lᴏʀᴅ is my portion; therefore I will wait for him." The Lᴏʀᴅ is good to those whose hope is in him, to the one who seeks him; it is good to wait quietly for the salvation of the Lᴏʀᴅ. . . . Though he brings grief, he will show compassion, so great is his unfailing love. For he does not willingly bring affliction or grief to anyone.
Lᴀᴍᴇɴᴛᴀᴛɪᴏɴs 3:22–26, 32–33

....
....
....
....
....
....
....
....
....
....
....
....
....
....
....
....

When I'm waiting on God, prayer takes more energy and work than usual. But the Bible has been my saving grace. When God seems silent on the other end of my prayers, His Word is the cord that keeps us connected and helps me find His voice. When my path weaves down into the darkness of "the valley of the shadow of death" (Psalm 23:4 KJV), the Bible is "a lamp for my feet, a light on my path" (Psalm 119:105).

Find the passages that fix you, that save you, while you wait. Let them serve as your road map through the lonely, unmarked waiting territory. Carry them with you. Write them on your fridge, your mirror, your hand, your heart. Read them over and over until you believe them and their message sinks deep down into your soul and changes you—even heals you. Begin compiling a list of go-to verses for this waiting season. Start by listing three scriptures that remind you of God's goodness and love. You might also list verses about God's faithfulness, the power of perseverance, and your status as God's beloved child.

As a father has compassion on his children, so the L<small>ORD</small> has compassion on those who fear him; for he knows how we are formed, he remembers that we are dust.
P<small>SALM</small> 103:13–14

....

....

....

....

....

....

....

....

....

....

....

....

....

....

....

....

....

When difficulty comes, God hurts with us. Just as a parent suffers when a child goes through a painful time of growth, so He suffers with us, His children.

How does it feel to know that God hurts when you hurt?
How does it change the way you feel toward Him when you pray?

....

....

....

....

....

....

....

....

....

....

....

....

....

....

....

....

....

....

....

*Bring joy to your servant, Lord, for I put my trust in you. . . .
Teach me your way, Lord, that I may rely on your faithfulness;
give me an undivided heart, that I may fear your name. . . . Give me a
sign of your goodness, that my enemies may see it and be put
to shame, for you, Lord, have helped me and comforted me.*
Psalm 86:4, 11, 17

....

....

....

....

....

....

....

....

....

....

....

....

....

....

....

....

....

$\mathcal{S}$ometimes when we are waiting for the life we want, we forget to enjoy the life we already have. It may be incomplete and imperfect (and keep in mind, *everyone's* life is incomplete and imperfect!), but it's still a life. *Your* life. God's gift to you. Don't just sit around waiting for the life you want; fill the days you have. Try new things. Take new risks. Remain social. Get out of the house. Keep your life fun and interesting.

What fun or exciting things would you like to try during this waiting season? Are there any trips you'd like to take? Hobbies you'd like to pursue? New skills you'd like to develop? List some ideas here.

....

....

....

....

....

....

....

....

....

....

....

....

....

....

....

....

*Guard me and deliver me; do not let me be put to shame,
for I take refuge in You. May integrity and what is right watch over
me, for I wait for You. God, redeem Israel, from all its distresses.*
PSALM 25:20–22 HCSB

....

....

....

....

....

....

....

....

....

....

....

....

....

....

....

....

....

....

*W*e all have seen waiting destroy people—steal dreams, harden hearts, strangle joy. It transforms their entire personality, making them bitter, envious, and jaded. They start stiff-arming the people who love them, and before long they are angry with God, alone in the crowd. They spend so much time asking *Why?* and *Why me?* and *How long?*—all questions without answers that lead only to anger and frustration—that they forget about the real issues, the questions they *can* answer, the answers they can choose: *How will I use this time?* and *Who will I become while I wait?*

How do you want to use this waiting time?
Who do you want to become while you wait?

You have searched me, Lord, and you know me. You know when I sit and when I rise; you perceive my thoughts from afar. You discern my going out and my lying down; you are familiar with all my ways. . . . If I rise on the wings of the dawn, if I settle on the far side of the sea, even there your hand will guide me, your right hand will hold me fast.
PSALM 139:1–3, 9–10

*E*xpanding your spiritual survival skills will help you survive your trek through the barren places, however long, however winding. Like Hannah, let's find courage to keep showing up to the places, people, and spiritual habits that can see us through day after day, month after month, even year after year.

What spiritual survival skills do you want to cultivate? Worship? Prayer? Fun? Self-reflection? Service? Laughter? How can you get started?

....

....

....

....

....

....

....

....

....

....

....

....

....

....

....

....

....

Let the light of your face shine on us. Fill my heart with joy when their grain and new wine abound. In peace I will lie down and sleep, for you alone, Lord, make me dwell in safety.

PSALM 4:6–8

....

....

....

....

....

....

....

....

....

....

....

....

....

....

....

....

Waiting seasons don't have to be lost time, and they don't have to be the end of you. You might even make some happy memories along the way. But you can't make memories if you don't *go make them*.

What memories would you like to make even while you wait?

....
....
....
....
....
....
....
....
....
....
....
....
....
....
....
....
....
....
....
....
....
....

In bringing many sons and daughters to glory, it was fitting that God, for whom and through whom everything exists, should make the pioneer of their salvation perfect through what he suffered. . . . For this reason [Jesus] had to be made like them, fully human in every way, in order that he might become a merciful and faithful high priest in service to God, and that he might make atonement for the sins of the people. Because he himself suffered when he was tempted, he is able to help those who are being tempted.

HEBREWS 2:10, 17–18

....

....

....

....

....

....

....

....

....

....

....

....

....

....

....

....

atan has a particular set of lies he has designed to torment us during waiting seasons. His deceptions target us where it hurts the most: insecurities in our relationship with God and insecurities about ourselves—our own spirituality, faithfulness, or worthiness.

As you wait, what insecurities are you facing in your walk with God? In your view of yourself? What scriptures can help you combat those insecurities?

....
....
....
....
....
....
....
....
....
....
....
....
....
....
....
....
....

"For my thoughts are not your thoughts, neither are your ways my ways," declares the Lord. "As the heavens are higher than the earth, so are my ways higher than your ways and my thoughts than your thoughts."

Isaiah 55:8–9

....

....

....

....

....

....

....

....

....

....

....

....

....

....

....

....

....

....

*G*od thinks differently than we do. Anytime we start playing the interpretation game, thinking things like, *God is doing this because He thinks. . .*or *This is happening because God wants. . .* , we should proceed with caution. Because unless God sends us a direct message from heaven, we are just guessing. We don't really know what God has in mind or why He does what He does. We can't know such things! During confusing times, we have to trust what the Bible tells us about God's nature, His grace, and His priorities, and choose to view our circumstances in light of those truths.

Make a list of some things you know to be true about God's character. Pair each truth with a Bible verse or an example from scripture whenever you can. (For example: God is kind: Psalm 103:13. God is gracious: Psalm 86:15.)

*Be merciful to me, L*ORD*, for I am in distress; my eyes grow weak with sorrow, my soul and body with grief. . . . But I trust in you, L*ORD*; I say, "You are my God." My times are in your hands.*
PSALM 31:9, 14–15

....
....
....
....
....
....
....
....
....
....
....
....
....
....
....
....
....
....

race. Don't be fooled by this short word, these five letters—so small, so unassuming—for *grace* may be the most powerful word in the world. God's grace can take our ugliest messes—harshest words, cruelest thoughts, most shameful deeds—and wash us clean. Not just it's-been-washed-but-I-can-still-see-the-coffee-stain clean. No, we get bright white, as-if-it's-never-been-worn clean.

God's grace is big enough.

God's grace lasts long enough.

God's grace never runs dry.

Waiting is not a punishment from God; it is a part of life. Everyone waits for things, even the most righteous of people.

In what ways have you needed God's grace during your wait?
How has God already shown you grace in your waiting?

"Which of you, if your son asks for bread, will give him a stone? Or if he asks for a fish, will give him a snake? If you, then, though you are evil, know how to give good gifts to your children, how much more will your Father in heaven give good gifts to those who ask him!"
MATTHEW 7:9–11

Satan tortures us with lies when we're waiting, lies like these:

God is making me wait because He is punishing me.

God is making me wait because He is mad at me.

God doesn't want me to be happy.

God is making me wait because He doesn't want me to have The Thing I want.

If I don't wait perfectly, God will never give me what I want.

Most of these statements put a lot of pressure on us and on our performance. We picture God up in heaven with His celestial red pen, marking papers, and we suspect He is secretly itching to put a big fat F at the top of the page. Every time we stumble or doubt, we panic: "Did I just cross the line and blow my chance? Now I'll never get that prayer answered!"

Which of Satan's lies do you wrestle with most? How does knowing that God is not angry with you, not punishing you, transform your view of God? Your view of waiting?

....

....

....

....

....

....

....

....

....

....

....

....

The Lord is compassionate and gracious, slow to anger, abounding in love. He will not always accuse, nor will he harbor his anger forever; he does not treat us as our sins deserve or repay us according to our iniquities. For as high as the heavens are above the earth, so great is his love for those who fear him; as far as the east is from the west, so far has he removed our transgressions from us.

PSALM 103:8–12

....

....

....

....

....

....

....

....

....

....

....

....

....

....

....

....

I can't read God's mind, but I do know what the Bible tells us about His character, and based on the picture the Bible paints, I can tell you this: God is not making you wait because He is angry. God is gracious, not one to hold a grudge. He speaks clearly when He wants us to change. He speaks through His Word, His people, and our consciences.

In what ways have you blamed yourself for your season of waiting? Describe a time when God has clearly shown you that it was time to make a change in your character. How did He make it clear?

....

....

....

....

....

....

....

....

....

....

....

....

....

....

....

....

....

....

I call as my heart grows faint; lead me to the rock that is higher than I. For you have been my refuge, a strong tower against the foe. I long to dwell in your tent forever and take refuge in the shelter of your wings.

PSALM 61:2–4

....

....

....

....

....

....

....

....

....

....

....

....

....

....

....

....

*S*atan's lies breed fear, mistrust, and discouragement. They make us insecure with God. Distant. Maybe even bitter. At a time when we most need our Father—we ache to curl up close and cry in His loving arms, to lie down and find rest in the protective shadow of His wings—we hesitate. We take a step back. Suspicion, guilt, and fear darken our view of God, damaging our trust. If the lies go unchecked long enough, we pull away. When that happens, Satan wins.

Your Father wants to walk your waiting days hand in hand, comforting you, lending you courage, carrying you when your strength gives out.

How has God carried you during your wait? If you have pulled away from God, what would it feel like to let yourself draw close to your Father again? To feel safe in His arms?

....
....
....
....
....
....
....
....
....
....
....
....
....
....

*Though I have fallen, I will rise. Though I sit in darkness, the L*ORD *will be my light.*

MICAH 7:8

....

....

....

....

....

....

....

....

....

....

....

....

....

....

....

....

....

....

God doesn't expect perfection. Of course, He is happy when we remain faithful, righteous, and close to Him (and when we do those things, we may experience some benefits, like peace and growth and joy), but God understands that we all struggle, and even fall flat, during our waiting times. God's biggest concern is that we *don't quit*.

Describe a time when you have fallen spiritually,
but God has shown you grace and helped
you find your footing again.

....

....

....

....

....

....

....

....

....

....

....

....

....

....

....

....

....

"Do not fear, for I have redeemed you; I have summoned you by name; you are mine. When you pass through the waters, I will be with you; and when you pass through the rivers, they will not sweep over you. When you walk through the fire, you will not be burned; the flames will not set you ablaze. . . . Since you are precious and honored in my sight, and because I love you, I will give people in exchange for you."

Isaiah 43:1-2, 4

$\mathcal{W}$e don't realize it, but we fall prey to misguided expectations, a sort of if-then theology:

If I am righteous, then God will bless me.
If I believe, then God will give me what I ask.
If I am a Christian, then my life will be happy.
More specifically. . .
If I don't flirt with worldly guys, then God will give me a godly boyfriend.
If I delight myself in God, then God will open my child's heart to Him.
If I pray with faith, then I will get well.

It's not that these if-then statements aren't true. It's just that they aren't *always* true. They aren't money-back guarantees. Waiting forces us to mature in our thinking. It makes us move past simplistic if-then theology.

Fill in the blank with some of the if-then thoughts
you have had during your wait:
If I _____, then God will _____.
If I _____, then God will _____.
What does God promise to His children, and how can
those promises bring you comfort as you wait?

....

....

....

....

....

....

....

....

....

....

*Trust in him at all times, you people; pour out your
hearts to him, for God is our refuge.*
PSALM 62:8

....

....

....

....

....

....

....

....

....

....

....

....

....

....

....

....

....

....

*G*od has devoted an entire book in His Word to prayers. When we read the book of Psalms, something in us rings with familiarity, echoes our own amen. The Psalms prompt our own prayers, offer words to borrow when we can't find our own. Listen as they whisper (and sometimes shout) your own fears. Find comfort in knowing you are not alone. Let the psalmists speak to your fears and give voice to your hurts.

Find a psalm that reflects how you feel about your waiting season and gives you the words you need to pray. Read the psalm in several Bible versions to give you a more complete understanding of its meaning. Pray through your psalm every day this week. There are many ways to pray through a psalm: You can simply read it to God. You can also read a verse or two, pause to add your own thoughts, then read the next verse, and so on, all the way to the end.

....

....

....

....

....

....

....

....

....

....

....

....

....

....

*How long, L*ORD*? Will you forget me forever? How long will you hide your face from me? How long must I wrestle with my thoughts and day after day have sorrow in my heart?*

PSALM 13:1-2

....

....

....

....

....

....

....

....

....

....

....

....

....

....

....

....

....

....

....

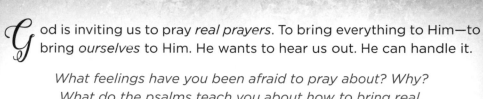

*G*od is inviting us to pray *real prayers*. To bring everything to Him—to bring *ourselves* to Him. He wants to hear us out. He can handle it.

What feelings have you been afraid to pray about? Why?
What do the psalms teach you about how to bring real,
raw feelings to God while maintaining a spirit of reverence?

....

....

....

....

....

....

....

....

....

....

....

....

....

....

....

....

....

....

....

....

Then Jesus went with his disciples to a place called Gethsemane, and he said to them, "Sit here while I go over there and pray." He took Peter and the two sons of Zebedee along with him, and he began to be sorrowful and troubled. Then he said to them, "My soul is overwhelmed with sorrow to the point of death. Stay here and keep watch with me." Going a little farther, he fell with his face to the ground and prayed, "My Father, if it is possible, may this cup be taken from me. Yet not as I will, but as you will."
MATTHEW 26:36–39

....

....

....

....

....

....

....

....

....

....

....

....

....

....

....

....

A "Gethsemane prayer" can be a turning point in our walk with God, when we learn to pour out our pain to God, to beg Him for what we want, but then humbly submit to His loving care. To trust that even if things stay hard or people make mistakes, God can set it right.

What attitudes do you need to surrender to God?
How can Jesus' prayer in the Garden of Gethsemane
help to guide your perspective and prayers?

....

....

....

....

....

....

....

....

....

....

....

....

....

....

....

....

....

....

....

But the eyes of the L<small>ORD</small> are on those who fear him, on those whose hope is in his unfailing love, to deliver them from death and keep them alive in famine. We wait in hope for the L<small>ORD</small>; he is our help and our shield. In him our hearts rejoice, for we trust in his holy name. May your unfailing love be with us, L<small>ORD</small>, even as we put our hope in you.
P<small>SALM</small> 33:18–22

....

....

....

....

....

....

....

....

....

....

....

....

....

....

....

....

....

When we are sad and frustrated and tired of waiting, how easy it is to forget to thank God. We have to *choose* to praise God for His kindness, generosity, and power. We have to *remember* to thank Him for gifts already given. If you are stuck in your walk with God, waiting for a blessing that won't come, try bringing gratitude and praise back into your prayer life.

For the next week, keep a gratitude list. Every morning,
look back on the day before and write down three
things you are grateful for. Thank God for each one.

....

....

....

....

....

....

....

....

....

....

....

....

....

....

....

....

....

*With the Lord a day is like a thousand years, and a thousand years
are like a day. The Lord is not slow in keeping his promise, as some
understand slowness. Instead he is patient with you, not wanting
anyone to perish, but everyone to come to repentance.*
2 Peter 3:8-9

....

....

....

....

....

....

....

....

....

....

....

....

....

....

....

....

....

*E*ven as you beg God for what you lack, make a point always to end your prayers with gratitude. That simple discipline will transform your perspective: Praise reminds us of His power; gratitude reminds us of His goodness. Together praise and gratitude protect our hearts and restore our hope.

How can you bring gratitude and praise back into your prayer life?
How might doing so protect or change your feelings toward God?
How might praise and gratitude transform your feelings
about where your life is right now?

....

....

....

....

....

....

....

....

....

....

....

....

....

....

....

....

"Are not two sparrows sold for a penny? Yet not one of them will fall to the ground outside your Father's care. And even the very hairs of your head are all numbered. So don't be afraid; you are worth more than many sparrows."

MATTHEW 10:29–31

....

....

....

....

....

....

....

....

....

....

....

....

....

....

....

....

*L*et's choose to fill our minds with God's playlist: scriptures and songs that fuel our faith and protect our relationship. God is not silent, as He sometimes seems; He has already given us His Word to tell us how He feels and how He works. It's up to us to use the Bible to fill in God's half of the conversation.

What scriptures can you add to your spiritual playlist, filling in God's half of the conversation? To get you started, here are a few of my favorites, all from Isaiah: 40:1–11; 40:27–31; 43:1–7.

....

....

....

....

....

....

....

....

....

....

....

....

....

....

....

....

....

In the same way, the Spirit helps us in our weakness. We do not know what we ought to pray for, but the Spirit himself intercedes for us through wordless groans. And he who searches our hearts knows the mind of the Spirit, because the Spirit intercedes for God's people in accordance with the will of God. And we know that in all things God works for the good of those who love him, who have been called according to his purpose.
Romans 8:26–28

....

....

....

....

....

....

....

....

....

....

....

....

....

....

....

....

*L*et prayer remain our refuge year after year, however long we wander in the waiting wilderness. Let us never give up on prayer, even when God feels far away. If we run out of words, let us sit and keep company with God, knowing that even in the silence He sees, He hears, and He cares. And when our waiting season ends, however it ends, let us celebrate with the One who has seen us through, heard us out, and never left our side.

Find a special place with God—a place you look forward to going to meet with your Father. A place where you can bring Him your heart— or where you simply sit in His presence, allowing the Spirit to speak the words you lack. Jesus had Gethsemane—where can you go?

....

....

....

....

....

....

....

....

....

....

....

....

....

....

....

....

....

Let us not become weary in doing good, for at the proper time we will reap a harvest if we do not give up.

GALATIANS 6:9

*G*od values persistence and perseverance; in fact, He calls us to them. . . . Time and again, God urges us to persist—in goodness, in hope, and especially in prayer.

Are you beginning to feel stupid asking God for the same thing over and over, day after day, for months or years on end? Don't. Are you wondering if God thinks you are being annoying or pushy or selfish? He doesn't. It's not wrong to be the squeaky wheel. Remember: God encouraged us to do it!

Do you think God wants to hear your persistent prayers, or do you secretly suspect you are annoying Him? What prayer do you want to revive (and repeat!) this week?

....

....

....

....

....

....

....

....

....

....

....

....

....

....

....

....

....

Draw near to God, and he will draw near to you.

JAMES 4:8 ESV

....
....
....
....
....
....
....
....
....
....
....
....
....
....
....
....
....
....
....
....
....
....
....
....

*P*rayer is no one-way conversation, however much it may sometimes feel that way. Our relationship with God involves give and take, and He cares about our opinions. God weighs our desires in light of His plans and our best interests, and sometimes He gives us what we want *because we asked*. Because He cares.

Do you view God as being flexible and approachable? Why or why not? How does it change your view of God to realize He wants to know how you feel—and what you want?

....

....

....

....

....

....

....

....

....

....

....

....

....

....

....

....

....

"Keep asking, and it will be given to you. Keep searching, and you will find. Keep knocking, and the door will be opened to you. For everyone who asks receives, and the one who searches finds, and to the one who knocks, the door will be opened."

MATTHEW 7:7–8 HCSB

We don't know what God has planned for our lives—will you get that promotion, that engagement ring, that healing?—because only God can answer for sure. But we do know that God welcomes our prayers—the repetitive, the heartbroken, the passionate—and He hears them. Though we are "but dust and ashes" (Genesis 18:27), our words matter. Our feelings matter. God takes our desires into account.

What have you been afraid to ask God for or pray about?

....
....
....
....
....
....
....
....
....
....
....
....
....
....
....
....
....
....
....
....
....

Relent, Lord! How long will it be? Have compassion on your servants. Satisfy us in the morning with your unfailing love, that we may sing for joy and be glad all our days. Make us glad for as many days as you have afflicted us, for as many years as we have seen trouble. May your deeds be shown to your servants, your splendor to their children. May the favor of the Lord our God rest on us; establish the work of our hands for us—yes, establish the work of our hands.

PSALM 90:13–17

When battles change us, even wound us, we can use our scars for good: they are reminders of God's power in our weakness. Memories of His care and concern. Marks that help us encourage friends in their sufferings: *I've been down in that dirt. It gets better from here.*

Let's wrestle in prayer. Roll in the dirt. Grapple and bleed.

Whatever God's final answer, we will be stronger for the struggle.

What blessings and scars has waiting given you? How might God one day use your scars to encourage others who have also suffered?

....

....

....

....

....

....

....

....

....

....

....

....

....

....

....

....

....

I will thank you forever, because you have done it. I will wait for your name, for it is good, in the presence of the godly.
PSALM 52:9 ESV

You never forget the people who wait with you, the friends who pray for you and with you. Who put up with you and your moods. Who listen to your rants, and still like you at the end of them. Who gently turn you back to God when you have turned the wrong way. Who still see the best in you even after you have revealed your worst.

Who is waiting with you in this season? In what ways would you like to bring God more into the center of your friendships?

....

....

....

....

....

....

....

....

....

....

....

....

....

....

....

....

....

....

And Saul's son Jonathan went to David at Horesh
and helped him find strength in God.
1 SAMUEL 23:16

*S*elflessness, sacrifice, and spirituality are things you and I can bring into *any* friendship. We can help one another find strength in God. We can pray together, point each other to scripture, and remind each other of God's promises. We can comfort each other, listen to each other, and we can simply show up and keep watch.

Would it help you to be more honest with a few friends about how your wait is going? If so, which friends, and what would you like to share with them?

*And I am sure of this, that he who began a good work in you
will bring it to completion at the day of Jesus Christ.*

PHILIPPIANS 1:6 ESV

*W*aiting can be intensely lonely. You feel like all your peers are moving forward—finding success, experiencing joy—while there you sit, stuck in neutral, or worse, reverse. At a time when we need friends more than ever, it's tempting to withdraw into our own struggle, convinced that no one relates, no one understands, no one cares. The longer we wait, the lonelier we may feel.

Waiting seasons have taught me to expand my support system. Even though some struggles may feel more private than others, I encourage you to take a risk. Let new people in. Open your heart to a few more confidants. You will be surprised by how many people love you enough to want to shoulder a part of your burden.

What are your fears or insecurities about being more open with friends and family about your struggles with waiting? What benefits might you reap from being brave in your current friendships— or being brave in opening up to new ones?

....
....
....
....
....
....
....
....
....
....
....
....
....
....

Let the word of Christ dwell in you richly, teaching and admonishing one another in all wisdom, singing psalms and hymns and spiritual songs, with thankfulness in your hearts to God.

COLOSSIANS 3:16 ESV

*T*he most satisfying friendships are the ones in which we let each other be ourselves. We embrace and enjoy each other, quirks, flaws, and all. We give a lot of grace. We call each other higher spiritually, we seek to grow together, and we are honest, but we also respect our differences and allow each other space and time to mature.

In what ways have your friends given you grace and space when you have needed it? How might you return the favor?

....

....

....

....

....

....

....

....

....

....

....

....

....

....

....

....

....

....

Make me to know your ways, O LORD; teach me your paths.
Lead me in your truth and teach me, for you are the
God of my salvation; for you I wait all the day long.

PSALM 25:4-5 ESV

....

....

....

....

....

....

....

....

....

....

....

....

....

....

....

....

....

$\mathscr{S}$ ome friendships come into our lives so that we can minister to each other for a time. This is especially true during waiting seasons, when we may connect with others suffering a similar health crisis or heartache. We comfort and support each other for a time, and when that time ends, our affection and memories remain, but our day-to-day time and attention may focus elsewhere. And *that's okay*. It doesn't mean the friendship was insincere; it just means that life sometimes takes us other places.

What friendships has God brought into your life just for a season?
Write what you appreciate about those friendships
here, and thank God for them.

....
....
....
....
....
....
....
....
....
....
....
....
....
....
....
....
....

*He said, "Surely they are my people, children who will be true
to me"; and so he became their Savior. In all their distress he too
was distressed, and the angel of his presence saved them.
In his love and mercy he redeemed them; he lifted
them up and carried them all the days of old.*
Isaiah 63:8–9

....
....
....
....
....
....
....
....
....
....
....
....
....
....
....
....
....

People can never occupy the God-shaped space in our hearts, no matter how thoughtful or devoted or almost-perfect they are. When we try to get people (even siblings or parents or best friends for life or even the love of our life) to become our *everything*, they will always fall short. We will still be left lonely. Why? Because only God is meant to be our everything.

How do you feel when you seek from people the things that
can only come from God? How can you more readily
rely on God to be your everything?

....

....

....

....

....

....

....

....

....

....

....

....

....

....

....

....

....

Each heart knows its own bitterness,
and no one else can share its joy.

PROVERBS 14:10

*P*eople—even the people who love us most—will not fully understand every nuance of what we feel while we are waiting. *That's okay.* Perfect understanding is God's job, not a person's job. When we are grieving, no one but God can fully feel our pain. When we are so singing-in-the-rain happy that we think our heart may explode, no one but God can fully feel our joy. God alone can hear our inmost thoughts; the Holy Spirit communicates our deepest desires to Him (see Romans 8:26–27).

How does it take pressure off your relationships when you stop expecting your friends to understand you perfectly?

....
....
....
....
....
....
....
....
....
....
....
....
....
....
....
....

For you are my rock and my fortress; and for your name's sake you lead me and guide me.

PSALM 31:3 ESV

*I*t's not wrong to share our lives with friends online—social media can provide powerful support—but if God is not *first* meeting our emotional needs, then social media will leave us feeling unsatisfied and vaguely lonely.

Want to feel closer to God emotionally?

Post less, pray more. Pray first, post last.

How might praying before posting—and praying more than you post— change the way you are handling your waiting journey? What changes have you already made in how you handle social media—or what changes do you want to make? Try this: Take a day or a week off of social media. (Breathe slowly, don't panic. You don't have to do this if you don't want to. Heh heh.) Take some time to journal afterward: How did you feel about your time away? What did you learn about yourself? How was your walk with God different? What adjustments do you want to make to your social media habits going forward?

....

....

....

....

....

....

....

....

....

....

....

....

....

The Lord said, "I have indeed seen the misery of my people in Egypt. I have heard them crying out because of their slave drivers, and I am concerned about their suffering."
EXODUS 3:7

_P_eople who love us will gladly offer a sympathetic ear and a shoulder to cry on as often as they can, but even so, everyone has limits. Our go-to person may not be available every time we need to talk; one single person can't carry our entire burden, however much he or she may want to. How can we protect our go-to relationship?

Go to God first. Go to God before you go to your go-to person! Share with God your grief, your joy, and everything in between. Let Him carry the lion's share of your emotions. Peter urges us, "Cast all your anxiety on him because he cares for you" (1 Peter 5:7). _All_ means _all_! Let's take God up on that promise.

> _How is your go-to relationship going? How can you tell if you are relying on them too much—or too little? What specific burdens do you need to cast on God today?_

The aim of our charge is love that issues from a pure heart and a good conscience and a sincere faith.

1 Timothy 1:5 esv

....

....

....

....

....

....

....

....

....

....

....

....

....

....

....

....

....

....

....

....

I have found that if I go into friendships with expectations, I get disappointed and hurt. The other person rarely meets my unspoken hopes. But if I go into a friendship to give, it's amazing how much I get back. Selflessness is a biblical principle: "Give, and it will be given to you. A good measure, pressed down, shaken together and running over, will be poured into your lap. For with the measure you use, it will be measured to you" (Luke 6:38).

Make a list of friends who are also going through a time of waiting or heartache, and begin praying for them regularly.

....
....
....
....
....
....
....
....
....
....
....
....
....
....
....
....
....
....

Give thanks in all circumstances; for this is
God's will for you in Christ Jesus.
1 THESSALONIANS 5:18

....

....

....

....

....

....

....

....

....

....

....

....

....

....

....

....

....

....

....

When we are waiting, we may feel cheated out of something we feel we deserve. Somehow, that can make us feel entitled to special attention and service from our go-to person, and chances are, he or she is happy to offer it. But let's be careful. Let's go out of our way to express love, affection, gratitude, and encouragement to friends and family who wait with us, realizing their devotion is a gift, not an obligation. A little thanks goes a long way.

Who do you need to thank today? Try this: Make a list of three people you'd like to thank. Find a way to express your gratitude this week: write a card, give a gift, or simply tell them in person how much you appreciate them.

....

....

....

....

....

....

....

....

....

....

....

....

....

....

"Do to others what you would have them do to you."

Matthew 7:12

....

....

....

....

....

....

....

....

....

....

....

....

....

....

....

....

....

....

When we are lonely, we might wish a new friend would just fall from the sky or move in next door. Once in a while someone new shows up, but chances are, you already have some great candidates for friendship in your life right now—at church, at work, in your neighborhood. Ask God to open your eyes and guide you.

If you need to expand your support system, where might you find some new people to whom you can open up your heart? How do you feel about putting yourself out there in some new relationships: Excited? Nervous? Intimidated?

....

....

....

....

....

....

....

....

....

....

....

....

....

....

....

....

....

....

Wait for the L<small>ORD</small>, and he will deliver you.
P<small>ROVERBS</small> 20:22 <small>ESV</small>

....

....

....

....

....

....

....

....

....

....

....

....

....

....

....

....

....

$\mathcal{H}$ow do you start opening up to new people if you aren't used to it? It's not as complicated as we make it. We open our hearts by opening our mouths. Share a detail or two and see what happens. Most of the time, openness prompts empathy and reciprocation.

What baby steps could you take to begin opening up a little more?
Could you. . .ask for prayer in your small group? Mention your wait to
a friend who doesn't yet know about your struggle? Invite a new
friend to have coffee? List some ideas here, and begin praying for
the courage and opportunity to put them into practice.

....

....

....

....

....

....

....

....

....

....

....

....

....

....

....

....

....

*The L*ORD *makes firm the steps of the one who delights in him; though he may stumble, he will not fall, for the L*ORD *upholds him with his hand. . . . The salvation of the righteous comes from the L*ORD*; he is their stronghold in time of trouble. The L*ORD *helps them and delivers them; he delivers them from the wicked and saves them, because they take refuge in him.*
PSALM 37:23–24, 39–40

*D*on't let envy alienate precious friendships. Let's pray to "rejoice with those who rejoice," just as we hope friends will mourn with us (Romans 12:15). Our turn for joy will come one way or another, and when that day comes, we still want to have friends left to celebrate with us!

While we are waiting, our friends may get jobs, get engaged, or get pregnant. That's okay. Our friendship can survive the challenge. Our friends might even get lost in their own happiness for a while, less sensitive to our heartache than they used to be (or maybe they are just uncertain of how to navigate the awkwardness). That's okay too. If we will give grace—the kind of grace they sometimes show us—the friendship can survive.

Take a moment to dream about the day you get to celebrate the end of your wait with your friends. (I know—it's scary to "go there." Okay, you can stop before your heart bursts.) Now. . .make a list of friends who have already received The Thing you are waiting for, and pray for those friends—thank God for the blessing they have received, and ask Him to direct their steps. (This practice protects your heart from bitterness and envy.)

*Rejoice in hope, be patient in tribulation,
be constant in prayer.*

ROMANS 12:12 ESV

*I*n the interest of sanity and self-preservation, we might have to let some friendships change during waiting seasons. While some friendships will become closer, others will need a little more breathing room. It might seem as if we are growing apart for a time, as our lives take different paths. We don't have to be rude or cut people off, but we might talk a little less frequently. They might not be our primary confidants in our struggle with waiting. If we are wise—not tossing friendships out the window or saying hurtful things, just dialing back their intensity a bit—we can still preserve the relationships and circle back to them when life settles.

Do you have any relationships that need some breathing room during this waiting season? What might that change look like, and how can you protect the relationship so you don't lose it altogether?

Love is patient, love is kind. It does not envy, it does not boast, it is not proud. It does not dishonor others, it is not self-seeking, it is not easily angered, it keeps no record of wrongs. Love does not delight in evil but rejoices with the truth. It always protects, always trusts, always hopes, always perseveres. Love never fails.

1 CORINTHIANS 13:4–8

....

....

....

....

....

....

....

....

....

....

....

....

....

....

....

....

....

When you're tempted to resent people who don't understand, keep this in mind: during our waiting times, our friends and family offer us grace *even though they don't understand*. They look past our crazy, and try to listen, to understand, to empathize. Let's offer them the same grace in return. Let's pay grace forward. We will cash in on the deposit before long.

We all have triggers during our waiting seasons: things people say that hurt us and make us angry. What are your triggers, and how do you respond when people set them off? How can you think differently or show grace when people make insensitive or ignorant comments?

And we know that all things work together for good to those who love God, to those who are the called according to His purpose.

ROMANS 8:28 NKJV

*M*y prayer for your waiting-season friendships is this: May you find friends wise enough to know when to speak and when to listen, when to confront and when to console, when to laugh-cry and when to just cry, when to commiserate and when to caffeinate. Above all, may they always come bearing chocolate. And when it's their turn, may you do the same for them.

Write your own prayer about waiting-season friendships in the space below. Ask God to strengthen your current friendships, provide the spiritual friendships you need, and help you be a selfless friend to others even as you wait.

....

....

....

....

....

....

....

....

....

....

....

....

....

....

....

....

Be strong, and let your heart take courage,
all you who wait for the Lord!
PSALM 31:24 ESV

....

....

....

....

....

....

....

....

....

....

....

....

....

....

....

....

....

....

....

I used to think I was the only one waiting for stuff, but gradually I came to realize that everybody is waiting for something. Even wealthy people and celebrities who don't seem to "need" anything. Even older people who appear to have life all figured out, all of their big life questions answered. Even that girl on Facebook with the great guy, 2.5 beautiful kids, 4,000 friends, granite countertops, and photos of her perfect family hitting life's milestones and highlights right on time.

Here's the truth: Nobody's life is perfect. Nobody has everything they want.

How does your perspective change when you realize that everyone is waiting for something? Listen more closely to your friends this week. What are they waiting for? What hard things are they going through?

....

....

....

....

....

....

....

....

....

....

....

....

....

....

"So you, by the help of your God, return, hold fast to love and justice, and wait continually for your God."

HOSEA 12:6 ESV

*L*ife may never be perfect (what is "perfect" anyway?), and it certainly won't go according to our five-year plan. But it can still be full. Meaningful. Godly. Rich. Even fun.

Here's another truth, one I have fought hard to embrace: we don't have to wait for perfect to find joy. The opposite holds true too: if we wait for perfect, we will never find joy.

Describe a time when you felt joyful even though life was imperfect. Now try this: write down three things that are going great in your life right now, and celebrate them in prayer.

....

....

....

....

....

....

....

....

....

....

....

....

....

....

....

....

....

*Ascribe to the L*ORD *the glory due his name; worship
the L*ORD *in the splendor of his holiness.*
PSALM 29:2

....

....

....

....

....

....

....

....

....

....

....

....

....

....

....

....

....

....

*S*ometimes we can't imagine feeling happy unless life comes in the exact packaging we have chosen for ourselves. *I'll never be happy until. . . I can't be content unless. . .* We have to get rid of the rules we set for our joy, the *until*s and *unless*es. This opens our heart up to enjoy gifts, even happiness, from God—even if they come in different forms than we had imagined.

Let's take a look at the rules we have set for our own joy.
Fill in the blanks with some of your own "rules":
I can't be happy until _____.
I won't be fulfilled unless _____.
My life doesn't count unless _____.
How can you rewrite those rules to allow yourself to reclaim
joy and contentment? Try these prompts to get you started:
I can be happy even while _____ because _____.
I can be fulfilled even though _____ because _____.
My life makes a difference for God and for people because _____.

Great is our Lord and mighty in power;
his understanding has no limit.

PSALM 147:5

No matter what you're waiting for, even if there is a hole in your heart where The Thing is meant to be, joy is still possible. Within reach. Even right here, right now—wherever *here* and *now* are for you, whatever they look like. Even without *it*—The Thing you are waiting for. Even if *it* turns out looking different than you had imagined.

How have you already experienced surprising joys during your wait?
What "unexpected ice cream" (unforeseen blessings that ease
the pain of waiting) have you received from God?

*Yet I will wait patiently for the day of calamity
to come on the nation invading us.
Though the fig tree does not bud
and there are no grapes on the vines,
though the olive crop fails
and the fields produce no food,
though there are no sheep in the pen
and no cattle in the stalls,
yet I will rejoice in the L*ORD*,
I will be joyful in God my Savior.*

HABAKKUK 3:16–18

....

....

....

....

....

....

....

....

....

....

....

....

....

....

*J*esus promised, "I have come that they may have life, and have it to the full" (John 10:10). A full life in Christ doesn't always include a picket fence, a handsome prince, or a perfect bill of health—at least, not all at the same time! Time and again, Jesus reminds us to look ahead for our happiness, ahead to heaven and the next life. To find our treasures, not in earthly things, but in things that will last in the life to come. Things that will not spoil or fade. In His few difficult years on this earth, He showed us how to find joy even in the midst of suffering and trial, imperfection and delay.

What do you most look forward to about heaven?

"Do not grieve, for the joy of the Lord is your strength."

Nehemiah 8:10

$\mathcal{W}$e can still choose joy, even while we are waiting, even when our life feels like one ginormous question mark. It won't be easy, and we may endure many painful, tear-soaked days before journey's end, but even so, we don't have to live in a constant state of suspended joy. We can experience happiness all throughout our waiting seasons.

How do you define being blessed by God? Even though you are waiting, how is God blessing you right now?

....

....

....

....

....

....

....

....

....

....

....

....

....

....

....

....

....

....

....

*And all the people gave a great shout of praise to the L*ORD*,
because the foundation of the house of the L*ORD* was laid. But many
of the older priests and Levites and family heads, who had seen the
former temple, wept aloud when they saw the foundation of this temple
being laid, while many others shouted for joy. No one could distinguish
the sound of the shouts of joy from the sound of weeping, because the
people made so much noise. And the sound was heard far away.*
EZRA 3:11–13

....

....

....

....

....

....

....

....

....

....

....

....

....

....

We can be happy and sad at the same time. Choosing joy doesn't mean the sad things in our lives have gone away. Choosing joy doesn't mean the grief, the loneliness, the depression, the sense of loss have disappeared altogether. As Proverbs 14:13 puts it, "Even in laughter the heart may ache." Life is rarely *all good* or *all bad*. Always, it's both.

How do you feel about the phrase "choose joy"? Write about a time when you have managed to hold on to some measure of happiness even when your heart ached.

....

....

....

....

....

....

....

....

....

....

....

....

....

....

....

....

....

And after you have suffered a little while, the God of all grace, who has called you to his eternal glory in Christ, will himself restore, confirm, strengthen, and establish you.

1 Peter 5:10 esv

*C*hoosing joy means we decide to find, appreciate, celebrate, and keep focus on the joyful things in our lives. The more we focus on those things, the more they ease some of our sadness, blunting grief's sharp edges, making it bearable. The sadness still hovers, but it fades further into the background, allowing positive feelings to sharpen and take primary focus. Loss becomes a dull and manageable ache instead of a crippling, all-consuming, somebody-bring-me-morphine-now crisis.

List five positive things you can focus on today.

....

....

....

....

....

....

....

....

....

....

....

....

....

....

....

....

....

We demolish arguments and every pretension that sets itself up against the knowledge of God, and we take captive every thought to make it obedient to Christ.

2 Corinthians 10:5

$\mathcal{W}$e start reclaiming joy by resisting joy killers: feelings, thoughts, and temptations that automatically bring us down. That means taming our thoughts, taking them captive and making them obedient to Christ.

List three joy-killing thoughts you've had recently (take them captive). Now try reframing or rephrasing those thoughts to allow for more faith (make them obedient to Christ). Next take those thoughts to God in prayer and leave them with Him.

....

....

....

....

....

....

....

....

....

....

....

....

....

....

....

....

That the genuineness of your faith, being much more precious than gold that perishes, though it is tested by fire, may be found to praise, honor, and glory at the revelation of Jesus Christ.

1 PETER 1:7 NKJV

....

....

....

....

....

....

....

....

....

....

....

....

....

....

....

....

....

*E*ven when life is good, going the way we want, happiness rarely just happens. Even in peaceful times, happiness is a choice. Our feelings are often the product of what we are thinking about, the perspective we choose to have.

What specific thoughts or truths can you focus on today that will help you to feel more grateful and joyful? (Try to write down at least three!)

....

....

....

....

....

....

....

....

....

....

....

....

....

....

....

....

....

But it is good for me to draw near to God.

Psalm 73:28 NKJV

....

....

....

....

....

....

....

....

....

....

....

....

....

....

....

....

....

....

$\mathcal{W}$e can sit around trying to resist the negative: *Don't be jealous of your friend's new job*; *Don't think that God is angry with you*; *Don't blame God for your disappointment. . . .* Or we can flood our minds with positive thoughts.

Philippians 4:8 gives us an extensive list of the kinds of things God wants us to fill our minds with: "Finally, brothers and sisters, whatever is true, whatever is noble, whatever is right, whatever is pure, whatever is lovely, whatever is admirable—if anything is excellent or praiseworthy—think about such things."

Make a list of things to think about today, things that are:
True: _____
Noble: _____
Right: _____
Pure: _____
Lovely: _____
Admirable: _____
Excellent: _____
Praiseworthy: _____
Whenever dark thoughts threaten, remind yourself
of these things in thought and in prayer.

....

....

....

....

....

....

....

....

....

....

"In the beginning, Lord, you laid the foundations of the earth, and the heavens are the work of your hands."

HEBREWS 1:10

When we are waiting, we can feel completely out of control—like our lives are spinning away in a direction we despise. But let us draw comfort from the knowledge that although we can't control *how long* we wait, we can control *how* we wait. Maybe we can't name the date we get better, get the raise, or get the break, but we can name the date we reclaim joy, and *it can be today*.

*How does it comfort and empower you to realize
you get to control how you wait?*

....

....

....

....

....

....

....

....

....

....

....

....

....

....

....

....

....

Rejoice in the Lord always.
Again I will say, rejoice!
PHILIPPIANS 4:4 NKJV

*M*ake joy and gratitude a deliberate part of your day. Start and end your day with a few minutes of directed thinking.

In the morning, write down:
- *three things you have to look forward to today or*
- *three things you are thankful for this morning.*

Before you go to bed, write down:
- *three positive things that happened today or*
- *three ways you saw God at work today.*

The Lord your God has blessed you in all the work of your hands. He has watched over your journey through this vast wilderness. These forty years the Lord your God has been with you, and you have not lacked anything.

DEUTERONOMY 2:7

....

....

....

....

....

....

....

....

....

....

....

....

....

....

....

....

....

....

When we are focused on ourselves and not depending on God, *we cannot see the good things God gives us*. We cannot see our blessings even when God drops them directly in our lap! Sometimes we are prospering *even while we wait*, but we are too focused on ourselves and our problems—too exhausted from the journey, too obsessed with what we *don't* have—to even notice what we *do* have, the other blessings God has already given.

Maybe God hasn't yet given you The Thing, but what other things
is He giving you to encourage you, boost your spirits,
and ease the pain of the journey?

....

....

....

....

....

....

....

....

....

....

....

....

....

....

....

"I will never leave you nor forsake you."

HEBREWS 13:5 ESV

....

....

....

....

....

....

....

....

....

....

....

....

....

....

....

....

....

....

....

....

....

*G*od doesn't value what the world values. The world values tangible blessings because those are all they have. Christians have so much more to look forward to. We can—and do—experience great blessings in this world, but we hold on to them lightly. We recognize the fragility and temporary nature of this life. Our true hope and greatest joys lie in the next world. Every joy here is but a shadow of the joys to come, a foretaste of eternity with God.

What does it mean to hold lightly to earthly blessings?
What spiritual blessings do you most appreciate? (Think about gifts like salvation, a clear conscience, a fresh start, ongoing forgiveness for daily blunders, the privilege of being God's child, meaningful relationships, membership in God's family, the hope of heaven. . .)

You are my hiding place; you will protect me from trouble and surround me with songs of deliverance.

PSALM 32:7

*W*e can't live in the land of *what if*, always worrying about what comes next, what could happen. To put this in scriptural terms, Jesus gently reminds us, "Do not worry about tomorrow, for tomorrow will worry about itself. Each day has enough trouble of its own" (Matthew 6:34).

Let's not give in to the temptation to play out long-term catastrophic scenarios: *What if I never get The Thing? What if life never changes?*

Let's take life the way God meant us to take it—one day at a time—treasuring small joys, thanking Him for providing the manna we need to make it through today.

How would it change your perspective and attitude if you stopped wondering "what if" and just enjoyed this day? What manna (small daily gifts) is God providing even now to see you through?

....

....

....

....

....

....

....

....

....

....

....

....

....

....

....

*Guide me in your truth and teach me, for you are God my Savior,
and my hope is in you all day long.*
PSALM 25:5

....

....

....

....

....

....

....

....

....

....

....

....

....

....

....

....

....

....

I nstead of thinking, *I have not found Mr. Right; therefore, it is safe to assume I will never find him, and I will die alone with my microwave dinners and cat collection,* why not think, *I have not found Mr. Right* yet? Why not think. . .

I haven't overcome anxiety yet.

I haven't gotten out of debt yet.

My child hasn't turned to God yet.

Yet is a powerful word. It makes room for hope and room for God. Three small letters, so much possibility.

*Try rephrasing some of your thoughts to leave
more room for hope—and God. Fill in the blanks:
I haven't received _____ yet.
I haven't overcome _____ yet.
I haven't seen God _____ yet.
How does your perspective change when
you phrase your desires like that?*

....

....

....

....

....

....

....

....

....

....

....

....

....

I remain confident of this: I will see the goodness of the Lord in the land of the living. Wait for the Lord; be strong and take heart and wait for the Lord.
Psalm 27:13–14

....

....

....

....

....

....

....

....

....

....

....

....

....

....

....

....

....

....

*M*ountaintop experiences—getting a promotion, getting engaged, buying a house, having a baby, moving to your dream city—don't come along that often in life. When they come, they are glorious, and we should stand on that mountaintop and praise the goodness of God at the top of our lungs. . . . But let's remember that most of life is lived between mountaintops, struggling from one peak to the next, with many dark valleys and rocky detours between. Life *is* the journey. And even as we hike, if we will stop and look around and live in the moment, we will be treated to breathtaking views.

What breathtaking views have you seen even during this period
of waiting? (Think about surprising blessings and
kindnesses shown by God or His people.)

....

....

....

....

....

....

....

....

....

....

....

....

....

....

"But now, Lord, what do I look for?
My hope is in you."
PSALM 39:7

*A*s you continue your journey through your waiting wilderness, try these simple decisions on for size:

- I choose to hold on to hope for the life I want, while choosing to find joy in the life I already have.
- I choose to keep praying for the blessings I want and need but to remain grateful for the blessings I already have.
- I choose to put life on pause. To notice the small treasures each day holds. To tuck them away in a secret place in my heart and draw them out again and again to remember the goodness of God, to relive His kindness, and to rejoice in the richness that's already mine.

Which choice in that list is the most difficult for you? Which is easiest? Why? What small treasures have you uncovered in your wait?

....

....

....

....

....

....

....

....

....

....

....

....

....

....

Then the disciples came to Jesus in private and asked, "Why couldn't we drive it out?" He replied, "Because you have so little faith. Truly I tell you, if you have faith as small as a mustard seed, you can say to this mountain, 'Move from here to there,' and it will move. Nothing will be impossible for you."

<small>MATTHEW 17:19–21</small>

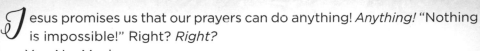esus promises us that our prayers can do anything! *Anything!* "Nothing is impossible!" Right? *Right?*

Yes. No. Maybe.

We have to be careful not to force Jesus' words into a super-literal box. What's the overall point of His words here? The big-picture message? Jesus' main point is not that we are guaranteed to receive *every blessing* we ask for in prayer if only we have enough faith—no, His main point is that there are no limits to the power of prayer when it is coupled with faith. To put it another way, prayer is powerful because *God* is powerful.

How have you experienced the power of prayer?

Take delight in the Lord, *and he will give you the desires of your heart. . . . Be still before the* Lord *and wait patiently for him.*
Psalm 37:4, 7

....

....

....

....

....

....

....

....

....

....

....

....

....

....

....

....

....

....

Our faith matters. Great faith, paired with God's power, can bring about awesome things. Anything God wants. On the other hand, a lack of faith can limit God's actions. Like it or not, our faith makes a difference.

Describe a time in your life when your faith was at its strongest. What made your faith so confident then, and how can you use that experience as a springboard to stronger faith now?

....

....

....

....

....

....

....

....

....

....

....

....

....

....

....

....

....

....

....

....

You need to persevere so that when you have done the will of God, you will receive what he has promised.

HEBREWS 10:36

....

....

....

....

....

....

....

....

....

....

....

....

....

....

....

....

....

....

....

*T*he relationship between our faith, our prayers, and God's will is complex and nuanced. Bottom line, we need to understand this: God is powerful enough to do anything—even hurl a mountain into the sea—but He always reserves the right to say no to our requests. He can do anything, but He is free not to do it. He is God; we are not.

List some examples of times when God told people in the Bible "no" or "wait." How did He use those answers to further His purposes?

....

....

....

....

....

....

....

....

....

....

....

....

....

....

....

....

....

....

*I have learned to be content whatever
the circumstances.*

PHILIPPIANS 4:11

$\mathcal{G}$od has already given us His best, and His best is all we need. He has given us His Son: "For God so loved the world that he gave his one and only Son" (John 3:16). He has given us Himself: "I am your shield, your very great reward," He told Abraham (Genesis 15:1). *God Himself* is our reward, and once we become Christians, we have Him, already and always. He is our Father, our Savior, our Friend.

When you meditate on the gift of God's precious Son—the best and most expensive gift He has to give—how does that change your feelings about your wait?

....

....

....

....

....

....

....

....

....

....

....

....

....

....

....

....

How blessed is God! And what a blessing he is! . . . (What pleasure he took in planning this!) He wanted us to enter into the celebration of his lavish gift-giving by the hand of his beloved Son. Because of the sacrifice of the Messiah, his blood poured out on the altar of the Cross, we're a free people—free of penalties and punishments chalked up by all our misdeeds. And not just barely free, either. Abundantly free! He thought of everything, provided for everything we could possibly need, letting us in on the plans he took such delight in making.

Ephesians 1:3, 5–9 msg

....

....

....

....

....

....

....

....

....

....

....

....

....

....

....

We have salvation, the Spirit, "every spiritual blessing" (Ephesians 1:3), "everything we need to live and to serve God" (2 Peter 1:3 EXB). Anything else, any blessing this side of heaven, is just gravy. The jobs, the family, the money, the comfortable lives we seek—while those are not necessarily sinful requests to make, they are bonuses. Let us learn the crucial difference in hoping for something given versus expecting something owed. The difference between a gift and a paycheck.

Have you ever secretly felt that God owed you a certain gift and was being stingy or unkind by withholding it? When did you feel that way and why? What scriptures can help to adjust your attitude?

I pray that the eyes of your heart may be enlightened in order
that you may know the hope to which he has called you,
the riches of his glorious inheritance in his holy people,
and his incomparably great power for us who believe.
EPHESIANS 1:18–19

$\mathcal{M}$aybe if we learn to look with different eyes, we will realize how blessed we *already are*. Because you don't yet have a husband, does that mean you are not richly blessed by your heavenly Father? Because I haven't yet gotten some career breaks I wanted, does that mean God is holding out on me? Because my father-in-law has been fighting cancer off and on for nearly twenty years, does that mean he is not living in God's favor? I say no. God says no. Even as we wait for God to answer some of our requests—even the deep-rooted desires that affect our identity and daily happiness—I pray we learn to recognize, and gratefully enjoy, the blessings He has already bestowed.

Fill in the blanks:
I am richly blessed by God because _____.
I know I am loved by God because _____.
I know God is with me because _____.

O L<small>ORD</small>, be gracious to us; we wait for you.
Be our arm every morning, our salvation in the time of trouble.

I<small>SAIAH</small> 33:2 <small>ESV</small>

....

....

....

....

....

....

....

....

....

....

....

....

....

....

....

....

....

....

....

....

*A*s we make requests of God, let's keep in mind that His goals are bigger than our temporary comfort. He prioritizes holiness above happiness. It's not that God is opposed to joy or that happiness in itself is somehow wrong (I really, really like being happy!); it's just not God's primary goal.

How is your wait helping you to become more holy?
(Or if you are still working your way through the Fighting God Stage,
how might your wait help you to become more holy in the future?)

....
....
....
....
....
....
....
....
....
....
....
....
....
....
....
....
....
....

*For through the Spirit, by faith, we ourselves eagerly
wait for the hope of righteousness.*

GALATIANS 5:5 ESV

*O*pen your eyes to see and your heart to embrace the promises that *are* there, that *are* true. The promises you can always rely on, even in darkest of times:

Not worldly wealth, but spiritual, emotional, and relational riches.

Not a problem-free life, but strength and comfort and shelter to see you through problems when they come.

Not everything you want every time, but everything you need without fail.

What is your favorite promise from scripture? Write it here,
and ask God to bring it to fruition in your life.

You will keep in perfect peace those whose minds are steadfast, because they trust in you. Trust in the LORD forever, for the LORD, the LORD himself, is the Rock eternal.

ISAIAH 26:3–4

....

....

....

....

....

....

....

....

....

....

....

....

....

....

....

....

....

The temptation, during waiting times, is to do absolutely nothing. To sit around twiddling our thumbs, playing mind-numbing games on smartphones or absently scrolling through friends' Instagram pictures, envying the productive and meaningful lives everyone else seems to be leading, just biding our time. Waiting.

But unless we want to spend our entire waiting season living life on pause, hiding in the corner, we have to work past the *until*s and *unless*es. We have to live in spite of the *if only*s.

What distractions have you filled your time with during your wait?
What changes do you want to make in the way you
spend your time and energy?

....
....
....
....
....
....
....
....
....
....
....
....
....
....
....

Therefore if you have any encouragement from being united with Christ, if any comfort from his love, if any common sharing in the Spirit, if any tenderness and compassion, then make my joy complete by being like-minded, having the same love, being one in spirit and of one mind. Do nothing out of selfish ambition or vain conceit. Rather, in humility value others above yourselves, not looking to your own interests but each of you to the interests of the others.

PHILIPPIANS 2:1–4

....

....

....

....

....

....

....

....

....

....

....

....

....

....

*A*s long as we are in the waiting room, we have decisions to make:
How will I wait?
How will I use this time?
Who do I want to be during this waiting season?
How can God use my life even now?

Record your answers to the questions above in the space below.

....

....

....

....

....

....

....

....

....

....

....

....

....

....

....

How long, LORD? Will you hide yourself forever? How long will your wrath burn like fire? Remember how fleeting is my life. For what futility you have created all humanity! Who can live and not see death, or who can escape the power of the grave? Lord, where is your former great love. . . . Praise be to the LORD forever! Amen and Amen.
PSALM 89:46–49, 52

....

....

....

....

....

....

....

....

....

....

....

....

....

....

....

....

....

One of the most frustrating things about waiting seasons is feeling that we have no control over our situation. (And let's be honest: feeling out of control is pretty much the worst feeling ever for every woman on earth.) *In theory* we understand that we are never fully in control of our lives, but waiting seasons bring us face-to-face with our own humanity, our own limits. The longer we wait, the more helpless we feel.

But I have good news! We do control one thing even while we are waiting: we control *how we wait*.

Describe how you feel when you realize you are not in control. How do you feel when you ponder the fact that you can control how you wait?

....

....

....

....

....

....

....

....

....

....

....

....

....

....

....

....

"Let your light shine before others, so that they may see your good works and give glory to your Father who is in heaven."

Matthew 5:16 esv

....

....

....

....

....

....

....

....

....

....

....

....

....

....

....

....

....

....

....

$\mathcal{W}$e have a choice:
A choice in how we think.
A choice in how we feel.
A choice in how we act.
A choice in how we spend time.
A choice in who we become.

What will you choose? List some specific thoughts, feelings, actions, occupations, and characteristics you want to choose during this time.

....

....

....

....

....

....

....

....

....

....

....

....

....

....

....

....

....

....

That is why, for Christ's sake, I delight in weaknesses,
in insults, in hardships, in persecutions, in difficulties.
For when I am weak, then I am strong.

2 Corinthians 12:10

....

....

....

....

....

....

....

....

....

....

....

....

....

....

....

....

....

....

*H*ow can we use our in-between times? *Will* we use them? Or will we just coast along on cruise control, trying to survive? Trying not to think, not to engage, because it's just too painful?

Maybe instead of thinking of waiting journeys as time lost, time wasted, we can think of them as time *repurposed*. Time spent doing things we never would have gotten to do otherwise. We can use our waiting times as opportunities to develop new skills, try new things, go new places, enjoy unexpected detours and surprising scenery. No, those things might not be our first choice for this season of life, but they are still good choices and meaningful ways to spend time.

What great opportunities have you already experienced because of your wait? As your wait continues, how do you want to repurpose this time moving forward? What skills would you like to develop? What new experiences would you like to try?

*Behold, as the eyes of servants look to the hand of their master,
as the eyes of a maidservant to the hand of her mistress,
so our eyes look to the Lord our God, till he has mercy upon us.*
Psalm 123:2 esv

....
....
....
....
....
....
....
....
....
....
....
....
....
....
....
....
....

*Y*ou can take charge of your time in the waiting room. Not in a way that says, "Forget You, God, You're doing a terrible job, so I'm taking the reins, doing things my way," but in a way that says, "Satan, you want to ruin this stage of my life, but I won't let you. I'm using this time for good and for God!"

Did you catch that last part? We can make God really, really, over-the-top happy by using waiting seasons for Him.

How do you want to use your waiting season for God's bigger purpose?
In what new ways might you serve Him or His people as you wait?

....

....

....

....

....

....

....

....

....

....

....

....

....

....

....

....

"Whoever wants to save their life will lose it,
but whoever loses their life for me will save it."

Luke 9:24

....

....

....

....

....

....

....

....

....

....

....

....

....

....

....

....

....

....

*L*osing your life—giving yourself away, talents and time and heart and all—will save you in the end. In fact, it will save you even now! Losing your life by choosing to serve others during a bleak time in your life, even when you feel you have little to give, will fill up your empty spaces. It will take the edge off your pain, show you the way out of loneliness, and make you feel whole again, even when something (or someone) is missing. No, it won't be exactly the same as if you had The Thing, but it will help.

Even as you wait, even as you hurt, what people around you also need comfort? To whom can you be a friend?

....

....

....

....

....

....

....

....

....

....

....

....

....

....

....

....

....

A generous person will prosper;
whoever refreshes others will be refreshed.

PROVERBS 11:25

....
....
....
....
....
....
....
....
....
....
....
....
....
....
....
....
....
....
....

*C*hoosing self*less*ness instead of self*ish*ness is one of the best things we can do *for ourselves*! Why? Because the desire to have a job you love, a baby you love, a guy you love (who loves you back!)—those are all part of our God-given desire for meaning, purpose, love, and fulfillment. And giving helps us fill that God-given space. We are made to give.

If you have more free time than you wish you had, how and where can you devote some of that time to others? To God? What underused talents, hobbies, or resources could you share in some new or out-of-the-box way?

Who can list the glorious miracles of the LORD? Who can ever praise him enough? There is joy for those who deal justly with others and always do what is right. Remember me, LORD, when you show favor to your people; come near and rescue me. Let me share in the prosperity of your chosen ones. Let me rejoice in the joy of your people; let me praise you with those who are your heritage.
PSALM 106:2-5 NLT

....

....

....

....

....

....

....

....

....

....

....

....

....

....

....

....

*J*esus says, "With the measure you use, it will be measured to you" (Luke 6:38). So how generous will you be right now? Give generously. God always, always, always outgives us in the end.

Describe a time in your life when God has outgiven you.

....

....

....

....

....

....

....

....

....

....

....

....

....

....

....

....

....

....

....

....

"I will send the hornet ahead of you to drive the Hivites, Canaanites and Hittites out of your way. But I will not drive them out in a single year, because the land would become desolate and the wild animals too numerous for you. Little by little I will drive them out before you, until you have increased enough to take possession of the land."
Exodus 23:28–30

*S*ometimes God blesses His people little by little. We'd rather receive our blessings all at once, in one overwhelming windfall, but God says, *"Nope. Getting it all at once would hurt you more than help you. I'm going to give it to you gradually, to give you time to grow into the responsibility."*

Take a look at your life: Is God blessing you little by little, even now? How?

*The LORD is good to all; he has compassion
on all he has made.*

PSALM 145:9

....

....

....

....

....

....

....

....

....

....

....

....

....

....

....

....

....

....

....

....

*W*hy not stop to notice and savor small blessings along the way? God might not be rescuing you from the waiting, but perhaps He is blessing you in other ways, filling your life with other joys. Pray to have an attitude that God *can* bless, and eyes to see the blessings He is already giving—even if they look different than the blessings you are praying for.

Write a prayer in the space below, asking God to help you see and enjoy the blessings He's already giving you.

....
....
....
....
....
....
....
....
....
....
....
....
....
....
....
....
....

This is love: not that we loved God, but that he loved us and sent his Son as an atoning sacrifice for our sins. . . . And so we know and rely on the love God has for us. God is love. Whoever lives in love lives in God, and God in them. This is how love is made complete among us so that we will have confidence on the day of judgment: In this world we are like Jesus. There is no fear in love. But perfect love drives out fear, because fear has to do with punishment. The one who fears is not made perfect in love.

1 John 4:10, 16–18

*H*ere's another way to take back control as we navigate the waiting wilderness: let's decide who we want to be during this time. We don't get to choose what happens *to* us, but we get to choose what happens *in* us. We choose *who we become*.

We can choose bitterness or gratitude.
We can choose selfishness or selflessness.
We can choose inertia or productivity.
We can let this time frustrate us or fuel us.

What have you chosen lately?
Have you felt frustrated or motivated by the wait?

....
....
....
....
....
....
....
....
....
....
....
....
....
....
....
....
....

Not that I have already obtained all this, or have already arrived at my goal, but I press on to take hold of that for which Christ Jesus took hold of me. Brothers and sisters, I do not consider myself yet to have taken hold of it. But one thing I do: Forgetting what is behind and straining toward what is ahead, I press on toward the goal to win the prize for which God has called me heavenward in Christ Jesus.

PHILIPPIANS 3:12–14

*I*f you choose to grow in even one character trait—faith, confidence, selflessness—during your waiting season, then your suffering has not been wasted.

What character trait or traits have you already grown in?
What one characteristic would you like to grow in?

....

....

....

....

....

....

....

....

....

....

....

....

....

....

....

....

....

....

....

*Having gifts that differ according to the grace
given to us, let us use them.*

Romans 12:6 esv

James 4:8 encourages us, "Come near to God and he will come near to you." When we take a step in a spiritual direction, God takes a step too—in *our* direction. When we make godly choices, God is right there, cheering us on and giving us strength. We are not alone.

Who do you want to be and become during this time? (Think about words like peaceful, grateful, kind, selfless, faithful, positive, prayerful, serving, mature, active, productive, open, honest, strong, realistic, fun.) What scriptures can help you develop those strengths?

....

....

....

....

....

....

....

....

....

....

....

....

....

....

....

....

....

....

Never be lacking in zeal, but keep your spiritual fervor, serving the Lord.
Romans 12:11

$\mathcal{D}$on't underestimate the power of decisions you make in the middle of your journey, in the places between. Maybe you feel like you're on an endless road trip right now, to places uncharted, a future unknown. The road stretches on past the horizon, unmarked and seemingly endless, curves without end.

We all get to choose how we navigate no-man's-land. We may yet be long miles from the place where we want to end up, but we can redeem the time. When the trip ends and the car door opens at last onto new soil, we will smile as we set foot in a new place. We might stretch unused muscles and kiss the ground, relieved to be free from the cramped car, but let's hope we can look back on those road-trip hours with some happy memories, knowing we are stronger now than we were at the start.

*What one decision would you like to make now,
in the middle of your journey? How will that decision
change your "road trip" for the better? Fill in the blanks:
My waiting season would not feel wasted if _____.
I already have some happy memories from
this time. They are: _____.*

....

....

....

....

....

....

....

....

....

....

*I will sing of your love and justice, L*ORD*. I will praise you with songs. I will be careful to live a blameless life—when will you come to help me? I will lead a life of integrity in my own home. I will refuse to look at anything vile and vulgar. I hate all who deal crookedly; I will have nothing to do with them. I will reject perverse ideas and stay away from every evil. I will not tolerate people who slander their neighbors. I will not endure conceit and pride.*

PSALM 101:1–5 NLT

....

....

....

....

....

....

....

....

....

....

....

....

....

....

....

*L*et's take back this time.
Let's use it for God instead of letting it go to waste.
Let's give what we have as we wait for what we want.
Let's not waste the wait.

What do you have to give today?
How can you ensure that you won't "waste the wait"?

....

....

....

....

....

....

....

....

....

....

....

....

....

....

....

....

....

....

When You did awesome works that we did not expect, You came down, and the mountains quaked at Your presence. From ancient times no one has heard, no one has listened, no eye has seen any God except You, who acts on behalf of the one who waits for Him.

Isaiah 64:3–4 HCSB

....

....

....

....

....

....

....

....

....

....

....

....

....

....

....

....

....

Waiting precedes miracles.
Sometimes waiting *forces* miracles. But a miracle is not a miracle without a wait.

What miracles have you already experienced in your life?
How long did you have to wait for those miracles to come about?

....

....

....

....

....

....

....

....

....

....

....

....

....

....

....

....

....

....

....

You hem me in behind and before, and you lay your hand upon me.
Such knowledge is too wonderful for me, too lofty for me to attain.
Psalm 139:5–6

....

....

....

....

....

....

....

....

....

....

....

....

....

....

....

....

....

....

$\mathcal{E}$ ven when we don't receive the miracle of *yes*, we still receive *other miracles* through waiting. Smaller, subtler miracles. They might not have fireworks and fanfare, but they are miracles nonetheless.

The smallest diamond is still a jewel.

Have you experienced any "small miracles"
during your wait? Describe them here.

....

....

....

....

....

....

....

....

....

....

....

....

....

....

....

....

....

....

There is no fear in love. But perfect love drives out fear.

1 John 4:18

....

....

....

....

....

....

....

....

....

....

....

....

....

....

....

....

....

When you wait, if you dare to share your struggles with friends—even when they are embarrassing, even when you'd rather keep them to yourself—you open yourself up to receive care and kindness. You find out how much people love you, how much they have to give. You find goodness in unexpected places.

Describe a time when you were vulnerable with a friend and they met your vulnerability with kindness.

Thank God, the Father of our Lord Jesus Christ, that he is our Father and the source of all mercy and comfort. For he gives us comfort in our trials so that we in turn may be able to give the same sort of strong sympathy to others in theirs. Indeed, experience shows that the more we share Christ's suffering the more we are able to give of his encouragement. This means that if we experience trouble we can pass on to you comfort and spiritual help; for if we ourselves have been comforted we know how to encourage you to endure patiently the same sort of troubles that we have ourselves endured. We are quite confident that if you have to suffer troubles as we have done, then, like us, you will find the comfort and encouragement of God.

2 Corinthians 1:3–7 Phillips

....

....

....

....

....

....

....

....

....

....

....

....

....

*W*ant to know one of the amazing blessings you might experience as a result of your waiting seasons? The ability to comfort others who are going through a similar trial. The ability to sympathize—and strongly. The wisdom to pass along the comfort God Himself has given you.

How has your wait taught you to empathize with others in new ways? How has waiting made you more compassionate, gracious, or patient with other people?

....

....

....

....

....

....

....

....

....

....

....

....

....

....

....

....

....

....

We may be mutually encouraged by each other's
faith, both yours and mine.

ROMANS 1:12 ESV

....

....

....

....

....

....

....

....

....

....

....

....

....

....

....

....

....

....

$\mathcal{H}$ow can your story help others? The more open you are about your own struggles, the more you will be able to minister to others when the time is right. You may not be ready now, but maybe one day, when you are traveling a more peaceful leg of your journey, you'll find words to share. Stories to tell. Comfort to pass on. You will look back with a jolt of joy and think, *God is using my loss for good*.

Even if you aren't ready to share it now, what part of your story do you look forward to sharing with others one day? How might your suffering one day help someone else?

No discipline seems pleasant at the time, but painful. Later on, however, it produces a harvest of righteousness and peace for those who have been trained by it. Therefore, strengthen your feeble arms and weak knees.
Hebrews 12:11–12

....

....

....

....

....

....

....

....

....

....

....

....

....

....

....

....

*L*earning and *becoming* might not sound like fun enterprises. Even if they aren't always fun, they are fulfilling. Rewarding. Growth is how we partner with God to make life count, give time purpose. We are not just twiddling our thumbs, waiting for something to happen. While we wait, we are *actively becoming* the people God wants us to be, people we will be proud to be at the end of our days.

How do you feel when you are actively growing in your character and faith? What growth are you most proud of?

....

....

....

....

....

....

....

....

....

....

....

....

....

....

....

....

....

....

God is not unjust; he will not forget your work and the love you have shown him as you have helped his people and continue to help them. We want each of you to show this same diligence to the very end, so that what you hope for may be fully realized. We do not want you to become lazy, but to imitate those who through faith and patience inherit what has been promised.

HEBREWS 6:10–12

....

....

....

....

....

....

....

....

....

....

....

....

....

....

....

....

$\mathcal{W}$hen we make decisions to grow spiritually, God meets us halfway, stepping in to help the heart change happen.

What are you most struggling with while you are waiting?

- *Simple impatience?*
- *Discouragement?*
- *Self-pity?*
- *Resentment?*
- *Envy?*
- *Embarrassment?*
- *A feeling of inadequacy compared to friends who already have what you want?*
- *Questioning God's love?*
- *Questioning God's ability to change your situation?*
- *All of the above?*

....
....
....
....
....
....
....
....
....
....
....
....
....

Now that we know what we have—Jesus, this great High Priest with ready access to God—let's not let it slip through our fingers. We don't have a priest who is out of touch with our reality. He's been through weakness and testing, experienced it all—all but the sin. So let's walk right up to him and get what he is so ready to give. Take the mercy, accept the help.

HEBREWS 4:14-16 MSG

....

....

....

....

....

....

....

....

....

....

....

....

....

....

....

*T*he temptations and questions we wrestle with show us where we can grow. Don't pressure yourself to master All the Things all at once; just pray about them and start addressing them one by one, little by little. Let the Bible guide your thoughts, your heart. Open up to godly friends about your struggle.

What struggles have most frustrated you in your wait? Which temptation would you like to focus on first? Do you think God will be patient with you as you seek to grow?

....

....

....

....

....

....

....

....

....

....

....

....

....

....

....

....

....

When my heart was grieved
and my spirit embittered,
I was senseless and ignorant;
I was a brute beast before you.
Yet I am always with you;
you hold me by my right hand.
You guide me with your counsel,
and afterward you will take me into glory.
Whom have I in heaven but you?
And earth has nothing I desire besides you.
My flesh and my heart may fail,
but God is the strength of my heart
and my portion forever.
PSALM 73:21–26

....

....

....

....

....

....

....

....

....

....

....

*I*f God drew us a map of our lives' journeys, tracking all our detours and delays, most of our maps would be a mess. Our maps would probably show long years spent wandering, circling back, meandering some more, repeating paths, hitting dead ends, off-roading, getting stuck, ditching the car and hiking for a while. . .because life is messy.

Life rarely takes the most direct, time-efficient route.

Life isn't a movie script, written to be resolved in two hours with a satisfying happy ending and no loose ends.

Life is long. Life is surprising. Life is confusing.

Sometimes life takes us places we don't want to go: sickbeds, crosses, tombs.

Sometimes God stands outside the tomb and holds us while we cry. Mingles His tears with ours.

And sometimes—oh, glorious day—He flashes a grin, rolls up His sleeves, and wakes up the dead.

How might you be different at the end of this season in your life—more pleasing to God, more like His Son, no matter the final outcome on your prayer? If God says no, can you imagine your life differently? If God says yes, how will you come back to praise Him?

....

....

....

....

....

....

....

....

....

....

*Therefore, wait for Me—this is the L*ORD*'s declaration—until the day I rise up. . . . On that day it will be said to Jerusalem: "Do not fear; Zion, do not let your hands grow weak. Yahweh your God is among you, a warrior who saves. He will rejoice over you with gladness. He will bring you quietness with His love. He will delight in you with shouts of joy."*
ZEPHANIAH 3:8, 16–17 HCSB

....
....
....
....
....
....
....
....
....
....
....
....
....
....
....
....
....
....

$\mathcal{A}$t journey's end, I pray you look back and say, "I'm better because of the wait." Better. Stronger. Closer. Humbler. More prayerful. More faithful. More confident. More compassionate. More selfless. More grateful.

At journey's end, I pray you lift hands to heaven, tears in your eyes and praise in your heart, and say, "It was worth the wait."

What do you want to say at the end of your wait?

....

....

....

....

....

....

....

....

....

....

....

....

....

....

....

....

....

More Inspiration and Encouragement for Your Waiting Season. . .

When God Says "Wait"

Author Elizabeth Laing Thompson invites you to walk alongside people of the Bible who had to wait on God. . .imperfect heroes like David, Miriam, Naomi, Sarah, Joseph, and others. Their stories will provide a roadmap for your own story, helping you navigate the painful, lonely territory of waiting, coming out on the other side with your faith, relationships, and sense of humor intact. They might even help you learn to enjoy the ride.

Paperback / 978-1-68322-012-1 / $14.99